Gillian

The Young Builder

J·A·W·S

Illustrated by
Gary Rees

Series editor: Rod Nesbitt

Heinemann Educational
a division of Heinemann Publishers (Oxford) Ltd
Halley Court, Jordan Hill, Oxford OX2 8EJ

Heinemann Educational Boleswa
PO Box 10103, Village Post Office, Gaborone, Botswana
Heinemann Educational Books (Nigeria) Ltd
PMB 5205, Ibadan

LONDON EDINBURGH PARIS MADRID
ATHENS BOLOGNA MELBOURNE
SYDNEY AUCKLAND PORTSMOUTH (NH)
SINGAPORE TOKYO

British Library Cataloguing in Publication Data
A catalogue record for this book is available from the British Library

ISBN 0 435 892371

Printed and bound in Great Britain by
Cox & Wyman Ltd, Reading, Berkshire

93 94 95 10 9 8 7 6 5 4 3 2 1

For Robert

Contents

Chapter One

Sipho's father was a builder, and Sipho loved building. He talked about building to his father when he was home. He thought about building in class and at break. He dreamed of the day he would build houses of his own.

Sipho was at school now. He was secretly building a house out of blocks. It was a very special house, with red bricks and a grey slate roof. It was his own house. His bedroom was already up to ceiling height. This was going to be his favourite room. It was large and it had a big window.

His father was always telling him that he had the perfect build for a builder. He was tall and thin, with long legs and arms for stretching and reaching. He had strong hands, but Dada had trained them for delicate jobs too. He could cut bricks, hang door frames and fit tiles just as well as he could dig or lay bricks.

'You've good strong hands, Sipho,' Dada said, 'but they're clever hands. You'll be a great builder one day.'

He wished he could concentrate on his building, but Maam Kuzwayo kept turning round from the chalkboard. Then he had to put his blocks down on the seat beside him and pretend to be writing in his exercise book.

Luckily, she was very busy with the chalk today. She was writing up a long list of new words. Sipho had plenty of time to balance his blocks, make windows with matches and Prestik, and cut the sticks he used for roofing materials. His desk partner, George, had been absent all week, so Sipho had taken a tray from home and put it on the seat beside him. This was a perfect place for his building construction.

He was just about to put in a window when Sizine whispered sharply from behind him.

'Master builder! How about doing some real work?' she said.

She leaned forward and pushed him hard. His blocks fell noisily on to the floor. Maam Kuzwayo turned round at once. Sipho stared at the blocks, then she marched up to his desk.

'Sipho,' she boomed, 'you're building again.'

Sipho sat still. He hated Sizine for getting him into trouble again.

'I've had enough,' said Maam Kuzwayo angrily. 'You never listen in class. You're always building.'

Sipho sat very still. He looked at the desk, hoping she would go away.

'Go to the Principal immediately,' she said, pointing to the door.

She leaned forward and pushed him hard.

There was no use arguing with Maam Kuzwayo. He got up and walked to the door. What would Maam Dime do this time?

When he got to her office, he stood outside the door for a long time. He looked up at the lettering. It said

PRINCIPAL
Shaningwi Primary School

Only yesterday he had stood in this same place. Maam Dime wasn't going to be very pleased. She could be very fierce. Her large arms would shake when she was angry. Sometimes she lost her temper, and she would lash out with a long ruler. She expected the very best from all the learners in her school. To her laziness was the worst crime. She had all kinds of punishments for learners who handed in careless work or who didn't concentrate in class.

Sipho knocked very softly, but the telephone rang just then, and Mrs Dime did not hear him. He stared at the door. He saw that it was slightly open. It was always slightly open. He looked more closely. The wood was badly warped. That was why it wouldn't close. It needed a carpenter to take some wood off the edge of the door.

He heard Mrs Dime put the phone down. He

felt like running away, but he knocked again, this time more loudly.

'Come in,' Mrs Dime called.

Shaking with fear, he walked into the office. Mrs Dime looked up.

'It's you,' she said, sounding very angry. 'You've been building in class again, haven't you?'

'Yes, Maam,' he said politely, but he could feel his legs trembling.

He remembered the last time he had been in her office, just yesterday. She had shouted at him and threatened to send him home if he played around in class again.

'Sit down, Sipho,' she commanded.

He obeyed quickly, because his legs were really shaking now.

'You don't have to be afraid,' Mrs Dime said. 'I'm just going to talk to you about your work.'

He couldn't believe it. She was going to be nice to him today! She didn't look at all fierce now.

'You haven't been doing any work at school, Sipho,' she said. 'Is something wrong?'

A picture flashed into his mind of his father's steamroller, a huge machine which rolled the earth over and over again until it was hard. He saw the piles of bricks and cement waiting at the site. Soon the bricklayers would be working with their

'You've been building in class again, haven't you?'

trowels, laying bricks as fast as they could. He would be helping too. There were only two more days to Saturday, the best day of the week, when he went to do real building work with his father.

'Sipho, I asked you a question,' Mrs Dime said loudly, making him jump. 'Why aren't you working? You don't listen in class, you don't do your homework, and you get bad marks in tests.'

'I'm sorry, Maam,' he said quietly. He couldn't think of anything to say.

'That's no answer,' she said. 'Your mother tells me she wants you to be a teacher.'

'Yes, Maam, but …' he said, thinking of the houses, schools and hospitals he was going to build when he left school.

'I know your father wants you to be a builder,' Mrs Dime said. 'But you won't build anything if you can't add and you can't write good English.'

Sipho smiled. Dada had a calculator. Often he pressed the buttons for his father when they worked out the cost of building materials together. And Dada never wrote any letters or anything. His mother did all that.

'I'll have a secretary!' he said, trying to sound confident.

'And the secretary will know more than the

boss!' Mrs Dime exclaimed. 'That's not a very good idea.'

Sipho didn't know what to say.

'What are we going to do with you, Sipho?' Mrs Dime sighed.

'Let me build,' he wanted to shout, but he just stared at the books on Mrs Dime's desk.

'I've tried punishing you, giving you lines, keeping you in after school, making you dig in the garden, but nothing seems to work.' Mrs Dime watched Sipho with a worried look on her face. 'I think it's time I talked to your parents. This has gone on too long.'

Oh no! There was enough of that at home.

'Sipho, do your homework,' his mother would say.

'Sipho, I want to show you something,' Dada would say, putting building plans on the table.

'You'll have to work very hard to be a teacher,' his mother would add.

'I'm going to make you the best builder in the world,' Dada would say, handing him a trowel and watching him put mortar on a brick.

Mrs Dime didn't waste any time. She looked at a list on her desk, picked up the telephone and dialled a number.

'Hello. Mrs Monde? This is Mrs Dime here. I

would like to make an appointment to see you and your husband. It is about Sipho's school work. Yes, I would like Sipho to be there. At home? Yes. At six o'clock this evening? I'll see you then. Goodbye.'

She put down the phone. Sipho waited.

'You can go now, Sipho,' she said. 'I'll see you tonight. At home with your mother and father.'

Maam Dime at his house!

A meeting with his mother and father!

And she expected him to be there!

He could pretend to be sick.

Or he could fall off his bicycle on the way home.

Why not visit George?

Maam Dime was always telling them to think of other people. If he visited a sick friend, surely she couldn't get angry with him. He would stay with George for hours and hours, and then he could pretend he had forgotten the time. When he came home, Maam Dime would have gone.

But that was no use. She would only come another day. He would just have to see her. He felt sick as he walked back to the classroom. Everyone was looking at him, wondering what punishment Maam Dime had given him this time.

'What did she do?' Sizine whispered as he sat down.

Sipho ignored her, but he could hear her talking to Pumla.

'Your mother can be really angry,' Sizine said. 'I think he's in trouble.'

Pumla said nothing. She didn't like her friends to talk about her mother.

'It's not nice being the Principal's daughter,' Pumla had told Sipho one day. 'I wish I went to another school.'

Sipho felt sorry for her. He wouldn't like it if people were rude about his mother.

Sipho didn't hear a word for the rest of the lesson. He was pleased when the bell rang. He wanted to think. He still didn't know what to do after school. He walked into the playground and sat down on a bench.

Sizine and her friends came into the playground. They stood in a circle around Pumla. He couldn't hear what they were saying, but they were asking her a lot of questions. Pumla shook her head and waved them away. She even pushed someone, but they would not leave her alone. Suddenly Sizine pointed at Sipho. Pumla shook her head again, but Sizine held her hand and pulled her towards Sipho. The other girls followed, giggling to one another.

'Go on, ask him,' ordered Sizine.

Pumla looked very unhappy.

'Go on!' said Sizine. 'He won't bite you.' She patted Pumla on the back.

'It's got nothing to do with you,' Pumla said angrily.

'I want to know,' Sizine shouted. 'Go on, I dare you to ask him.'

Pumla looked as if she was going to cry.

'Ask me what?' Sipho said, trying to help her. She smiled at him.

'Just what punishment you got,' she said quickly.

'Oh that!' he said. 'Maam Dime's coming to my house, that's all.'

'What a punishment,' laughed Sizine. 'That will teach you to play with baby's blocks in class.'

Sipho got up quickly.

'I was just practising for the real building on Saturday,' he said.

'You'll turn into a brick one of these days,' Sizine laughed. 'Thick brick!' She laughed again and pointed at him.

'You're jealous because you can't come to the building site with me,' he replied.

'You don't think I want to go there, do you?'

'That's because you're too scared,' Sipho laughed. 'You're frightened a brick would fall on you.'

'That's not funny,' she said.

'Bang would go all your brains,' Sipho went on, feeling silly now.

But that was the only way to make Sizine stop. If you were nasty to her, she left you alone.

'You can talk,' she said. 'What did you get in your last test?'

'Oh go away and leave him alone,' said Pumla.

'Thick brick,' Sizine shouted again. 'You're not worth talking to. Let's see if the Principal's daughter can put some sense into his thick head.'

She walked off with her friends. They giggled and laughed to one another. Sipho watched as they disappeared into the classroom.

'I want to see you building,' Pumla said softly.

Maam Dime's daughter wanted to see what building was like! What would her mother say? Sipho smiled. It would be nice to take her to the building site, but he didn't think Maam Dime would allow her to go.

'Your mother will think it's too dangerous,' he said.

'No, she won't,' Pumla replied. 'She'll say it's good for me. It's educational, something new. Please, can't I come with you?'

'Maybe,' Sipho said.

He was much too shy to show how pleased he was. She really wanted to come with him.

'Oh go away and leave him alone,' said Pumla.

'It would be good fun,' she said, smiling.

He thought so too, but he couldn't tell her he would like her to come.

'I'll ask my father and tell you tomorrow,' he said, trying not to show his excitement.

He walked quickly away before she noticed how pleased he was. He just hoped the Principal would allow Pumla to go to the building site. She was good fun to be with and she was very pretty too. She had a lovely smile and a beautiful slim figure. She looked just as pretty as the girls in magazines.

But it didn't really matter if she wasn't allowed to come. Soon he would be at the building site with his father, and that was more important than anything else. Maam Dime and his mother could talk all they wanted. He was going into the real world to make a real building and nothing could stop him.

Or that was what he thought!

Chapter Two

The first thing Sipho noticed when he walked into the house was the smell of something burning. It was coming from the kitchen. That wasn't good. His mother would be in a bad mood.

He was right. She was very angry about Maam Dime's visit, so angry that she had forgotten to take two cakes out of the oven. They were so badly burnt that even the dog would not eat them.

'Mrs Dime is coming to see us this evening, Sipho,' his mother said.

'Yes, Mama,' he said.

'She wants to talk to us about your work. Do you know that?'

'Yes.'

'It's all this building you're doing. You'll never be a teacher if you think about bricks and … and concrete mixers all the time.'

'Maam Dime doesn't like me,' Sipho said.

'Don't be silly,' his mother replied. 'She doesn't want you to be lazy, that's all.'

Sipho thought of digging foundations, pouring concrete, of laying bricks carefully in a straight line.

'Dada's not lazy,' he said quietly.

'No, he's not lazy,' Mama laughed. 'He wasn't lazy at school either.'

'Who isn't lazy?' asked Sipho's father, walking into the kitchen at that moment. He sniffed. 'Is something burning?'

'We're talking about how hard you work,' said Mama, going to give him a kiss. 'Not like Sipho. Mrs Dime's coming this evening to talk about his school work.'

'Will we take her out to the building site on Saturday, Sipho?' laughed Dada. 'Then she can see how hard you work.'

But then his father looked very serious.

'But you must do your homework too,' he said. 'You must pass your exams or you'll be in Standard Five for ever. Then you can never be a builder!'

Sipho put his hand over his mouth. Dada was right. They would make him write the same exam over and over again. Instead of being out on the building site, he would be adding and subtracting and learning spellings. Yes, he would have to work harder.

At that moment there was a knock at the front door.

'It's for you, Sipho,' his mother said, smiling.

Maam Dime!

It was all right seeing her in her office, but to see her at home, with his parents listening. He couldn't move.

'Go on, Sipho,' said his mother, 'open the door.'

Dada gave him a pat on the back and pushed him gently.

'Go on, be a man,' Dada said in a very deep voice.

Sipho smiled. Dada always tried to make things better.

'I'll be brave,' Sipho said in a deep voice, just like Dada's.

He felt much happier now. He even smiled at Maam Dime when he opened the door.

'Hello, Sipho,' she said.

'Hello, Maam Dime,' he replied, still smiling.

'Are your mother and father at home?' she asked.

'Yes, Maam,' he said, leading her into the living room.

'Good evening, Mrs Dime,' Dada said in a polite voice.

'Good evening, Mr Monde.'

'Please sit down,' Dada said, pointing to the best chair. Mama came in from the kitchen with tea and a plate of sandwiches.

Sipho kept himself busy, handing out tea and giving everyone a sandwich. By the time he had finished, Mrs Dime had already told his parents what she thought about his school work.

Sipho kept himself busy, handing out tea.

18

'Well, Sipho,' she said, 'what are you going to do?'

Sipho looked at his father. Dada was looking very serious. He looked so serious that Sipho wanted to laugh. But he knew it would be silly to laugh in front of Maam Dime. Dada nodded his head to tell Sipho to answer Maam Dime's question.

Sipho took a deep breath and looked at Mrs Dime.

'I'm going to work harder, Maam.'

His mother looked pleased. But Mrs Dime did not even smile.

'That's not good enough,' she said. 'You told me that the last time.'

'I will, Maam, I promise,' he said quickly. 'I'll work really hard.'

'No, Sipho, it's no good making promises. I want results. How can we get results?'

Sipho looked at Mama this time. She was shaking her head and doing something with her hands. Sipho didn't know what she was trying to tell him. Mama moved her hands again. It looked as if she was putting one brick on top of another. Then she shook her head. No building! He couldn't tell Maam Dime that!

'How do you spend your weekends, Sipho?' asked Mrs Dime.

Now he was trapped. He didn't know what to say.

'He spends all day on Saturday with his father at the building site,' said Mama quite angrily.

'Oh, I see,' said Mrs Dime, nodding her head. 'So that's why he never does his weekend homework.'

'He's not just watching,' said Dada trying to help. 'He's very good. He … he digs foundations, lays bricks, paints, everything.'

'That's what he does in class,' Mrs Dime replied.

'Excuse me?' Dada said, looking puzzled.

'Mr Monde, your son Sipho spends all his time building. When he's not dreaming about building, he's playing with his blocks in class and annoying the other children.'

'Oh dear, that's bad,' was all Dada said.

Sipho was worried. He knew he was in big trouble. Even Dada couldn't save him from Maam Dime's punishment.

'Sipho, come here,' she ordered loudly.

Sipho almost dropped his sandwich, but he caught it and put it on a plate. Then, slowly, he walked over to her.

'I want you to stop all this building and concentrate on your school work,' she said.

He turned to Dada. Surely Dada would say something. But his father just sat looking worried.

'But …,' Sipho tried to speak.

'It's no use knowing how to build things if you can't do your school work properly,' she continued.

Still Dada said nothing.

'I think you should come to school on Saturdays and do all the work you've missed,' Mrs Dime said.

He couldn't! It wasn't fair!

'No!' he said. He didn't mean to sound rude, but he had to go to the building site with Dada.

Mrs Dime glared at him angrily. Nobody spoke to her like that.

'I can't,' he said, trying to make her understand.

'Just like you can't pass your tests?'

'Dada, help me,' Sipho shouted, but this time he didn't say the words out loud.

'Be at my office at nine o'clock on Saturday and we'll see how much work you can do,' Mrs Dime said. Then she stood up to go.

This was terrible. The classroom block was only half-finished. Dada needed him to lay the bricks. Why didn't Dada say something? He was just standing politely saying goodbye! Surely this wasn't happening. He felt as if he was going to scream. Maam Dime was walking towards the door. Surely Dada was going to stop her – or Mama? They didn't seem to care.

Dada got up and followed the Principal to the door. He was holding something in his hand. Maam Dime was just about to open the door when Dada put his hand on the handle. He was going to be polite and open it for her.

But Sipho was wrong.

'Mrs Dime,' said Dada, with his hand on the door handle, 'would you like to come and see the building site on Saturday. It's really very interesting. Some of the buildings are nearly finished and we are just starting some of the others. Your daughter could come too. It would be a new experience for her.'

Sipho couldn't believe it. Maam Dime had told him to come to school on Saturday, and Dada was asking her to come and see the building site.

'That would be very nice,' Mrs Dime replied, 'but Sipho and I have work to do.' She looked at the door.

'That's a pity,' Dada said. 'The inspector is coming on Saturday. You could see how everything has to be built correctly.'

She turned round again.

'There's an office at the site,' Dada went on. 'We can have tea. I think your daughter would like it.'

Sipho held his breath.

'It would be very interesting,' Mrs Dime said,

'Here's a map to help you find the way,' said Dada.

'and Pumla could learn a lot. But what about Sipho's school work?'

'He'll work tonight, and on Friday night. I'll see that he does all his homework – properly.' Dada was not smiling when he looked at Sipho.

Sipho stared at his father. He was making a bargain with Maam Dime, but Sipho could see that he was serious. School work and building or no building was what he was saying.

'Yes, Dada,' Sipho said. 'I'll really work hard.'

As he said the words, he knew they were true. If he wanted to go with Dada to the building site, he would have to work harder. Well that would make Mama happy too.

'I'll take you to the site on Saturday,' said Dada, 'but we'll have to leave early.'

'We'll come later,' Mrs Dime replied. 'I must do some work at school first.'

'Here's a map to help you find the way,' said Dada. He held out a piece of paper.

Sipho stared at his father. Dada had planned the whole thing. Maam Dime and Pumla were coming to the site. Now he could show them what a hard worker he was. Then they would know that Dada and he were the best builders in the world.

Chapter Three

Sipho loved getting up early on Saturday mornings. It was five o'clock and he was already making coffee and plates of toast. Dada called it their 'man's breakfast'.

'Man's breakfast ready?' Dada shouted.

'Yes, Dada,' Sipho replied.

'Good, we'll have to work hard this morning.'

Sipho put mugs and plates on the table and spread jam on a piece of toast. He started to eat quickly. His father came into the room.

'So Mrs Dime and Pumla will be watching us today,' Dada said. 'We must show them how hard we work.'

'I will,' Sipho said. 'I can't wait to get there.'

'Well, you deserve it,' Dada laughed. 'I've never seen you do so much homework in one night.'

'That's because I had to,' said Sipho.

'Yes, but if you want to do well, you have to work hard all the time.'

Sipho was eating his second piece of toast, but he was beginning to get impatient. He loved driving with Dada in the front of his big truck. It was so high you could see everything from up there. It was better than being at the top of a big tree.

Dada was drinking his second cup of coffee.

Sipho was beginning to get impatient.

When he had finished, he picked up his building plans and his diary.

'Ready?' he asked, taking the keys for the truck from their place on the wall.

'Ready!' Sipho said, jumping up.

'You open the truck while I say goodbye to Mama,' Dada said, giving Sipho the keys.

It was a long way to the school Dada was building. They had to go through town, along a narrow road, up a very steep hill and then along a dusty track before they got there. It took over an hour, which was why they had to leave so early. Dada stopped in town to get some pieces of wood. Sipho jumped out of the truck and watched them loading the heavy planks. He wanted to be tall and strong when he grew up. Then he would be the king of the builders.

The truck started off again. Sipho put on his safety belt and rested his head against the seat. He shut his eyes. The movement of the truck was making him sleepy. He wasn't used to working so hard on Friday nights. He sat very quietly and thought of all the places he had helped Dada to build. There was that school hall in town, the hospital, a beautiful house and now there was this new school. It was exciting to watch the buildings grow week by week. First they built the walls, then the roof and finally the doors and windows were put in. Sipho fell fast asleep. He woke up as the truck drove through the security gates at the new school.

He looked all around. There were three parts to the new school: the hall, the classrooms and the toilet block. While Dada went into the site office to talk to the foreman, Sipho ran to watch the earthmover lifting scoops of dark brown earth. There was dust everywhere. Some grit flew into Sipho's eye. He rubbed it. It was itchy and painful, but he quickly forgot about it. He loved the great machine. As it moved the whole world seemed to shake.

He went over to the classrooms. The walls of one of the blocks were quite high. Some of the workmen were just starting work on the other one. He watched a man hammering in stakes while another measured distances carefully. Some of the workmen were carrying picks and shovels. It was quite hot already and they had tied their shirts around their waists. Some women were braaiing boerewors and drinking water from plastic bottles. Sipho stood and watched them for a few minutes. But soon he went to the classroom block where the men were mixing mortar and starting to lay bricks. Dada was watching them. He was still talking to Mendele, the foreman.

'Some door-frames and window-frames were stolen last night,' Mendele said, looking very worried.

'How many?' asked Dada, running his hand through his hair.

'Nine door-frames and six window-frames,' replied Mendele.

Dada gave a big sigh.

'Show me what size they were,' said Dada, 'and I'll order some more.'

Mendele went over to the other classroom block. Dada and Sipho followed him. Sipho knew things were stolen from the site, but never as much as this.

The walls of the classrooms were up to roof height. Dada smiled when he saw this. He ordered one of the workmen to start putting up scaffolding to work on the roof.

'Keep away from the scaffolding, Sipho,' he said. 'I don't want you climbing on to it and falling off.'

'I want to help with the roof,' Sipho said.

'It's too dangerous,' Dada replied. 'No, I want you to lay some bricks.' He pointed to the other classrooms.

Sipho quickly got a trowel and a pile of bricks. Before Dada could turn round, Sipho was putting mortar on the wall and laying a brick on top of it.

He worked so hard that he didn't hear a car coming through the security gates. It was only when Mrs Dime was standing beside him that he saw her.

'Your father is right,' she said, 'you're an excellent bricklayer.'

Sipho smiled. Maam Dime had never praised him before. The word 'excellent' was used for people like Sizine. But then he saw Pumla looking at his dirty hands and the mortar on his overalls. He looked at his dusty shoes and wondered what she was thinking.

'Show Pumla how to lay a brick,' Mrs Dime said.

He had never seen anyone look so astonished before. Pumla couldn't believe what her mother had said.

'Come on, Pumla,' said her mother, 'try to lay a brick like Sipho does.'

Pumla looked very unhappy when Sipho gave her the trowel. He showed her how to take some mortar and put it smoothly on top of the wall. She tried to copy him, but her hands were shaking. When she had finished, the mortar was all uneven.

'Good try,' said Sipho, quickly smoothing the mortar. 'Now you put a brick on top of that. It's easy.'

Pumla looked scared. Her hands were shaking even harder. Sipho felt sorry for her. He showed her what to do with the brick. She smiled at him gratefully.

'Well done, Sipho,' Mrs Dime said, 'and thank you for showing Pumla.'

Sipho looked pleased. This was better than getting into trouble at school.

'You're a very good builder,' Mrs Dime said.

She had been so interested in his work that she had forgotten about Dada. She didn't see him standing watching them. She turned in surprise when Dada asked her to have some tea in the office.

'Thank you,' she said. 'Are you coming, Pumla?'

'I want to watch Sipho building,' Pumla replied. Sipho looked at her in surprise.

Mrs Dime stopped.

'Be careful,' she said, 'building can be dangerous.'

Sipho smiled to himself as she looked up at the men on the scaffolding.

'And don't trip over anything,' she said as she walked after Dada.

Pumla nodded, and then smiled at Sipho. She went over to the wall and ran her fingers over the bricks.

'It must be fun when you know how to do it,' she said.

She stood and watched as he began to build.

'I like it,' said Sipho, 'but I'm no good at school work.'

'You can't be good at everything,' Pumla said, laughing.

'But Mama and Dada want me to be good at school,' he said.

'Show me how you build,' she said quickly. 'I like it here.'

She stood and watched as he began to build. He loved to hold the bricks and work with the mortar. Soon he was so busy that he forgot that Pumla was there.

Chapter Four

Sipho laid a row of bricks and then stood back to look at his work.

'That's good,' said Mendele, coming over to see what Sipho was doing. 'Now you should take a rest. Show your friend the foundations for the other block.'

'You want to see?' asked Sipho, suddenly remembering Pumla.

She nodded, looking pleased.

Sipho took her past the classroom blocks and over to where the toilets would be built. The foundations were in deep ditches where Sipho loved to play. He liked to slide right to the bottom. The ground was far above him and he pretended he was in a castle. He could run around the foundations shouting war cries, shooting arrows and fighting battles. He could make as much noise as he liked and nobody got angry. But today he had a girl with him, and she wouldn't want to play war.

'Do people hide in there sometimes?' she asked.

'I don't know,' replied Sipho. 'It does look a good place to hide.'

'It looks very dark,' she said. 'There could be something horrible in there.'

'Don't be silly. Come on, let's go down.' He got ready to jump.

'I can't,' she said, sounding very frightened.

'Of course you can. It's easy,' Sipho said.

'It's too far,' she said, still looking down at the foundations.

'No it isn't. Look!' And he jumped into the hole.

'Come on,' he said, holding out his hands to her. 'Jump!'

'No,' she whispered.

'Come on. Look, I'll catch you,' he laughed, holding out his arms.

'All right then,' she said in a low voice.

She stood at the edge of the hole and shut her eyes tightly.

'Sit down and open your eyes,' he warned. 'Then you can see where you're going.'

But she didn't listen. She took a leap through the air and landed on one leg. She twisted her ankle and gave a sharp cry. When he bent down to help her, he saw that she was crying with pain.

He tried to work out how he was going to get her out of the hole. Maam Dime would be really angry.

'I can't walk,' she said, trying to stand on her foot.

'Oh dear,' said Sipho, 'I hope you haven't broken anything.'

'Oh dear,' said Sipho, 'I hope you haven't broken
anything.'

'I don't think so,' she said, looking at her sore ankle.

'Sit down and let me see your ankle,' said Sipho, trying to remember some of the first-aid he had learnt in health classes.

'Ouch,' she cried when he pressed her ankle.

'You've broken it,' Sipho said, very worried now.

'No, I think it's sprained,' she replied. 'It's not so bad now.'

He hoped she was right. Then he remembered that she was better at Health Science than he was.

'We'll still have to get some help,' she said.

Sipho wasn't ready to get help yet. He could climb out of the foundations easily. He had done it many times before. He could call for help and the workmen would come immediately. They would lift her on their shoulders and carry her out of the ditch. But then he would have to face Maam Dime.

'Be careful, building can be dangerous,' she had said.

Now Pumla was sitting in the foundations with a badly hurt ankle. And it was all his fault. He really was in trouble.

'Sipho, please call for help,' Pumla pleaded.

He could see that she was in pain, but he still didn't want to move. He wanted to hide here with Pumla and hope that no one would find them.

'Can't we just stay here for a few minutes,' he asked, sitting down beside her, 'and pretend you didn't hurt yourself?'

'You're scared!' she said, looking really surprised.

'What's your mother going to say?' he asked.

'Is that what you're worried about?' she said angrily.

'Of course I'm worried about your ankle too,' he said quickly.

'But you're more worried that my mother is going to kill you,' she laughed.

'What do you think she's going to do?' he asked.

'She'll probably give us both extra homework at the weekend to keep us away from building!' she said. 'She always said it was dangerous.'

'Now she knows it's dangerous,' Sipho sighed.

'What was that?' Pumla asked suddenly, sitting up straight.

'I didn't hear anything,' Sipho replied.

'Listen!' she said loudly.

'It's only the concrete mixer,' he said.

'No, there's something else,' she said quietly. 'It's quite close. I'm scared.'

'Where's the sound coming from?' Sipho asked.

'From behind us,' she replied, holding his arm.

Sipho listened very carefully.

'What can you hear?' he asked.

'It's a ticking sound, like the noise a clock makes,' she said. She looked scared. 'Maybe it's a bomb.'

'Don't be silly,' he replied.

'Sipho!' she cried.

'What?' he said.

'I know it's a bomb,' she shouted. 'Get me out of here, before it's too late.'

Now Sipho knew why she got all the best parts in the school plays. She could be so dramatic.

'Come on, Sipho,' she said, getting up and walking slowly towards the bank. 'Let's go.'

'Pumla, there's no bomb in here,' he said, kicking the sand. But that didn't stop her from screaming.

'Help! Help! A bomb! Get me out.'

One of the builders came running towards the foundations. He peered down at them.

'There's no bomb, silly,' laughed Sipho, holding up an alarm-clock which had been lying in the dirt.

By that time a crowd had gathered above them. Among the people peering down was Mrs Dime herself.

'What is going on down there?' she called. 'Are you all right?'

'A bomb,' muttered Pumla.

'It's just an alarm-clock,' said Sipho, holding up the clock.

'Oh,' gasped Pumla.

'Don't worry, there's no bomb,' said Sipho.

Then Pumla started to laugh. She laughed so much her whole body was shaking.

But Mrs Dime did not think it was funny.

'You'd better come out of there,' she said .

'I can't,' said Pumla, trying very hard to stop laughing.

'Why not?' asked her mother, beginning to sound very annoyed.

'I've hurt my foot,' Pumla replied.

'Oh dear,' Mrs Dime said. 'Is it bad?'

'No,' said Pumla, but she still couldn't walk properly.

'Does it hurt badly?' asked her mother.

'It's nothing,' she said, trying to climb out of the foundations. She was pulling herself up and standing on her good leg.

Immediately Sipho ran to help her. He pushed her from behind while one of the workmen pulled her arms. When she was safely out of the foundations, Sipho climbed up after her.

'We must get a bandage,' Mrs Dime said, sounding very worried.

Sipho ran off to the office to fetch a bandage

Sipho pushed her while one of the workmen pulled her arms.

from Dada's first-aid kit. He also took some ointment for sprains. Then he hurried back to Pumla. Mrs Dime put on some of the ointment and then bandaged Pumla's foot. Pumla soon felt much better. She stood up and limped to her mother's car.

Mrs Dime brushed the dust from her skirt. She was still looking very serious.

'I don't think this was a good idea after all,' she said.

'I'm sorry about Pumla's foot, Maam,' Sipho said. 'She jumped too quickly, and –'

'What was she doing jumping into those foundations?' Maam Dime asked angrily.

'She –'

'Listened to you,' Mrs Dime went on. 'And then you scared her with that alarm clock. Bomb indeed!'

'That wasn't my fault,' said Sipho. 'She –'

'You're a naughty boy, Sipho.'

Mrs Dime turned and walked angrily to her car.

Sipho sighed as he watched the car moving slowly over the bumps to the gate. That was the end of Pumla's visits to the building site.

And what about his work here? Maam Dime would give him so much homework after this. She was very, very angry about what had happened to Pumla.

'I don't want to go to school on Monday, Dada,' Sipho said when they were driving home. 'Can't you say I'm sick?'

'No, Sipho,' replied Dada firmly. 'You must go to school. You must show Mrs Dime that you're going to do your work.'

Sipho didn't enjoy the rest of the weekend. He was too worried about what was going to happen when he got to school on Monday.

Chapter Five

Early on Monday morning, the telephone rang.

'Sipho, it's for you,' called his mother.

Who could be phoning him at this time?

Maam Dime?

His heart was beating very fast as he picked up the phone.

'Hello, Sipho, it's Pumla.'

'Oh, hello Pumla,' he said, very surprised to hear her voice.

'Listen, my mother's still very angry. She says I can't go building with you any more.'

'I thought she would say that,' replied Sipho.

But he smiled to himself as he thought of Pumla's shaking hand as she tried to lay a brick.

'I want to come – every Saturday,' Pumla said. 'I want you to teach me about bricks and mortar. I like it out there with you.'

Sipho felt very happy, but then he remembered her sore ankle.

'How's your ankle?' he asked.

'It's not sore any more,' she said. 'It was just a little sprain.'

'Can you walk on it?'

'Yes, yes,' she said impatiently. 'My mother's still putting ointment and bandages on it, but it's going to be all right.'

'That's good,' sighed Sipho, feeling much better. But then he remembered Maam Dime.

'Your mother's still angry with me, isn't she?' he asked.

'She's angry, but it wasn't your fault. I was so silly, jumping like that.'

'What's she going to do to me?' Sipho asked in a worried voice.

'She's going to give you so much homework that you won't be going near the building site either.'

'Oh no!' he groaned.

'But stop worrying,' Pumla said. 'You can make her forget that she's angry with you.'

'How?'

'Her office door won't close. It makes her so angry. Can't you fix it quickly before school starts?'

'I'll have to get there soon,' said Sipho, looking at his watch.

'It will make her so happy,' said Pumla. 'She'll forget she's angry with you.'

'All right, I'll try,' he said.

'Who was that?' Mama called from the bedroom.

'It was Pumla,' he replied. 'I have to go to school very early to do some work.'

'I thought Mrs Dime would make you do that,' Mama said.

Sipho didn't tell her about the broken door. He quickly helped himself to some toast and a mug of tea. Then he grabbed his suitcase and said goodbye to Mama and Dada who were just getting up. He went into the garage. He took Dada's plane and slipped it into his suitcase. Dada wouldn't be angry, especially if he knew what it was for.

He ran through the school gates, looking around nervously. It was too early for the children, but sometimes teachers came in at this time. They marked their books and got ready for the school day. This morning there was nobody in sight.

He went straight to Maam Dime's office, put his suitcase on the floor and opened the door. He looked at the edge of the door which would not close. Then he closed the door as far as it would go and took out a pencil. He marked with the pencil the wood he would have to plane off. He was going to have to work very fast. He would also have to be very careful. He didn't want Maam Dime complaining about cold winds blowing into her office.

He started to work. He pushed the plane up and down the edge of the door. Small pieces of wood fell to the floor. Up and down he went. Up and down. There was a little pile of wood shavings on the floor now.

He felt the edge of the door with his hand. It was getting smoother.

Shave, shave, shave. Up and down, up and down. This was hard work. He would have to go faster.

What would Maam Dime say if she saw him planing her door? Maybe she would think he was trying to break it. He moved the plane faster and faster. Up and down, up and down. He was going to finish the job before Maam Dime came to the office.

After twenty minutes he tried to close the door. It still wouldn't close properly. He looked at his pencil mark. There was quite a lot more wood to shave off. He worked harder and harder.

At last he stopped for a rest. He looked at his watch. Seven o'clock. She would be here soon. He started again, planing as fast as he could. At the same time he tried not to make any mistakes.

He was just about to finish when Pumla limped up to him.

'Quick, she's coming,' she called.

There were wood shavings all over the floor. He pushed the plane up and down three or four more times and then put it back into his suitcase.

'Quick! Hide!' said Pumla. She opened the office

He worked harder and harder.

door and pushed him inside. 'In the cupboard.'

He stepped into the coat cupboard and she shut the door just as her mother walked in.

'What's going on?' Mrs Dime asked angrily, pointing at the mess on the floor. 'Has someone tried to break into the office?'

'Look, Mama,' said Pumla, closing the door carefully. 'Your door shuts properly now.'

'Goodness,' said Mrs Dime, smiling. 'Somebody's been working here.'

She went over to the door. She bent down and examined it.

'It's such a careful job,' she said. 'Only a real carpenter could do a job like that.'

She brushed at some of the wood shavings.

'But I didn't know anyone was coming! I wonder where he is?'

She opened the door and looked up and down the corridor. There was no one in sight.

'It was Sipho,' Pumla said. 'Only Sipho could do a job like that.'

'Sipho!' Mrs Dime said in surprise.

'Yes,' Pumla laughed, 'Sipho fixed your door.'

'But where is he?' Mrs Dime asked.

Pumla walked over to the cupboard. She stopped for a moment and then threw open the door.

'Sipho!' Mrs Dime said in amazement.

Sipho felt a fool as he stepped out of the cupboard. Pumla was so silly. Why had she opened the cupboard at all? He could have stayed there until Maam Dime left to go to assembly.

For a moment Mrs Dime said nothing. She stood and looked at Sipho.

What was she thinking?

What was she going to do?

Was he in trouble again?

Sipho waited. His legs began to shake.

Then Mrs Dime walked towards him. She was holding out her hand.

'Thank you, Sipho,' she said, 'thank you for fixing my door so beautifully. That door has made me angry for months. Now I can close it again.'

Sipho started to smile. She wasn't angry. She was pleased with him.

'I'll clean up the mess now, Maam,' he said. 'I have to get a broom.'

'Don't worry about that,' she replied. 'I'm so pleased I can close my door.'

'Can I go to the site with Sipho on Saturday?' asked Pumla.

'You can go when your foot is better,' her mother said. 'He can teach you all about building.'

'Oh, thank you,' Pumla said, looking at Sipho.

Then Mrs Dime walked towards him.

'Sipho,' Mrs Dime said, 'I know you will be a very good builder one day. But I want you to take care of Pumla when she's at the building site.'

'I will, Maam,' Sipho said. 'Thank you for letting her come.'

'But you must do your homework and work hard in school,' Mrs Dime said firmly.

'I will, Maam,' Sipho said, looking at the Principal. 'I know I have to work hard to be a great builder.'

As he left the Principal's office he thought of the buildings he had helped Dada to build. Then he dreamed of the buildings he was going to build himself. When he was a builder, he – . But he had to get there first. He had a lot of hard work ahead of him before he became a great builder, like Dada.

Questions

1 What did Sipho's mother want him to become when he left school? What did his father want him to become?
2 How did Maam Kuzwayo know that Sipho was playing with building blocks?
3 What punishment did Maam Dime give Sipho?
4 When Maam Dime came to Sipho's house, what did Sipho's mother signal that he should do?
5 How did Sipho get out of the punishment?
6 How did Sipho get into trouble at the building site?
7 What was his punishment for this?
8 How did Sipho escape this punishment?
9 At the end of the story what did Sipho realise he would have to do?
10 What did Sipho dream of doing?

Activities

1 Draw a picture of the house you would like to live in. Then draw a plan of the house (looking down on it from above), showing what rooms you would have in the house.
2 Write a short story about a small boy who falls into the foundations of a house. Describe what happens to him and how he is rescued.

Glossary

boerewors (page 28) large sausages

braaiing (page 28) cooking over an open fire

building plans (page 8) drawings of the building the builders are working on

concentrate (page 1) pay very careful attention to something

concrete (page 15) a mixture of mortar and small stones

dramatic (page 39) acting as if she was in a play

earthmover (page 28) a machine with a huge scoop at the front for lifting loads of earth

foundations (page 15) the concrete base a building stands on

mortar (page 8) a mixture of sand, cement and water used to hold bricks together

plane (page 46) a machine for smoothing wood

scaffolding (page 29) a metal frame put at the side of a building for workmen to stand on

site (page 5) the place where the building is going up

site office (page 28) a small office on the site for storing all the plans and other papers for the building

sprained (page 37) painful injury to a leg or arm caused by twisting

stakes (page 28) sharply-pointed pieces of wooden stick

trowel (page 7) small shovel for lifting mortar to help build walls

warped (page 4) crooked, not straight, caused by the sun

The Junior African Writers Series is designed to provide interesting and varied African stories both for pleasure and for study. There are five graded levels in the series.

Level 3 is for readers who have been studying English for five to six years. The content and language have been carefully controlled to increase fluency in reading.

Content The plots are linear in development and only the characters and information central to the storyline are introduced. Chapters divide the stories into focused episodes and the illustrations help the reader to picture the scenes.

Language Reading is a learning experience and although the choice of words is carefully controlled, new words, important to the story, are also introduced. These are contextualised, recycled through the story and explained in the glossary. The sentences contain a maximum of three short clauses.

Glossary Difficult words which learners may not know and which are not made clear in the text or illustrations have been listed alphabetically at the back of the book. The definitions refer to the way the word is used in the story and the page reference is for the word's first use.

Questions and **Activities** The questions give useful comprehension practice and ensure that the reader has followed and understood the story. The activities develop themes and ideas introduced and can be done as pairwork or groupwork in class, or as homework.

Resource Material Further resources are being developed to assist in the teaching of reading with JAWS titles.

Other JAWS titles at Level 3